THE GREAT ARTISTS

Édouard Manet

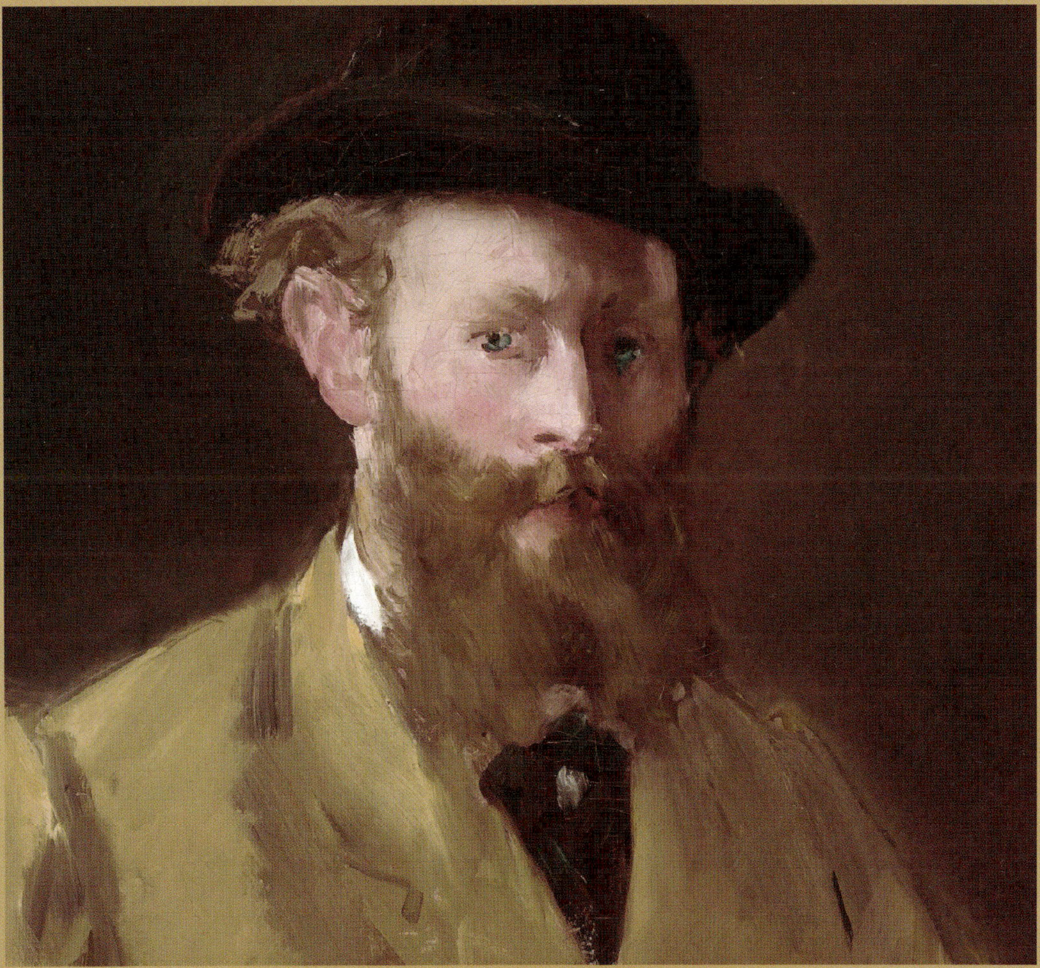

Anjali Raghbeer

Om KIDZ
An imprint of Om Books International

Manet loved walking through the streets around Montmartre in the late hours of the night when the city was wide awake in that part of Paris.

He noticed a rag-picker who collected used bottles.

He went up to him, 'Sir, do you mind if I paint you?'

The rag-picker laughed.

'Me? You must be out of your mind. No one will buy your painting,' he said.

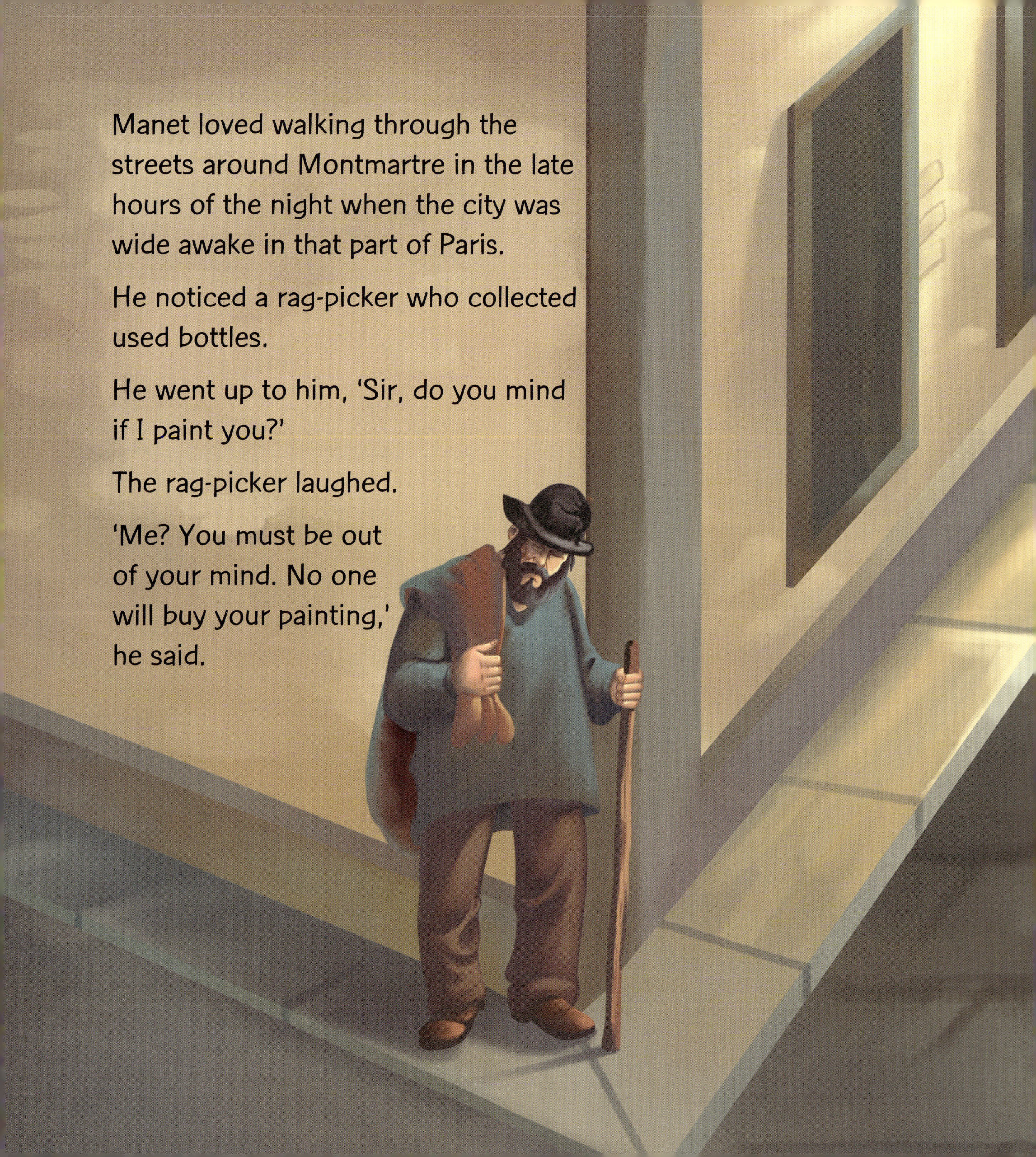

'I don't paint for money,' said Manet, he had grown increasingly frustrated with how people were only painting biblical or historical scenes. He wanted to do something new.

'Alright. How much will you pay me?'

Manet slipped a few francs into the man's hand.

'Every night, I will paint you right here,' said Manet and quickly set up his easel.

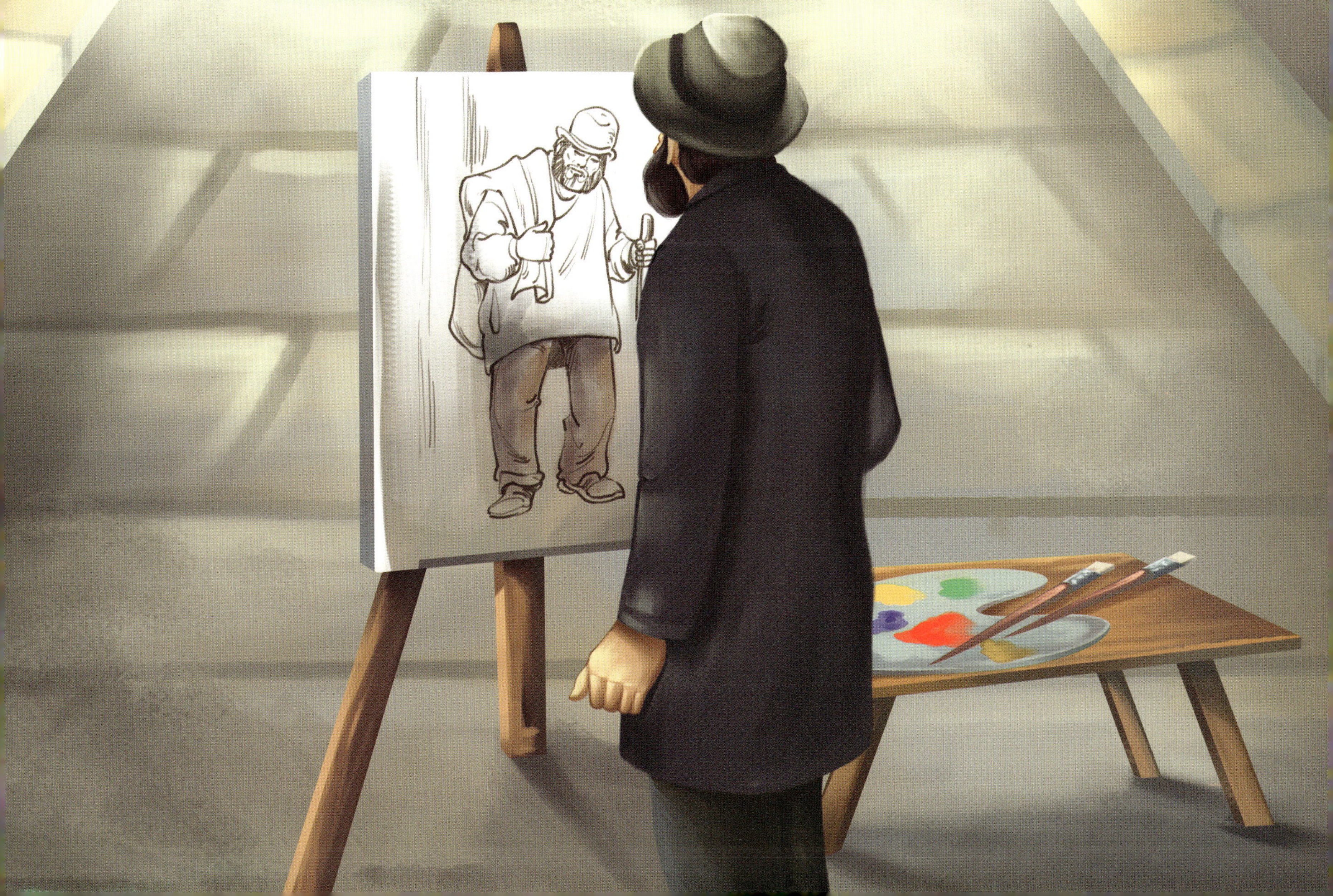

Manet was pleased with how the painting turned out. *The Absinthe Drinker* he called it. He was now even more sure that he wanted to paint people as they were.

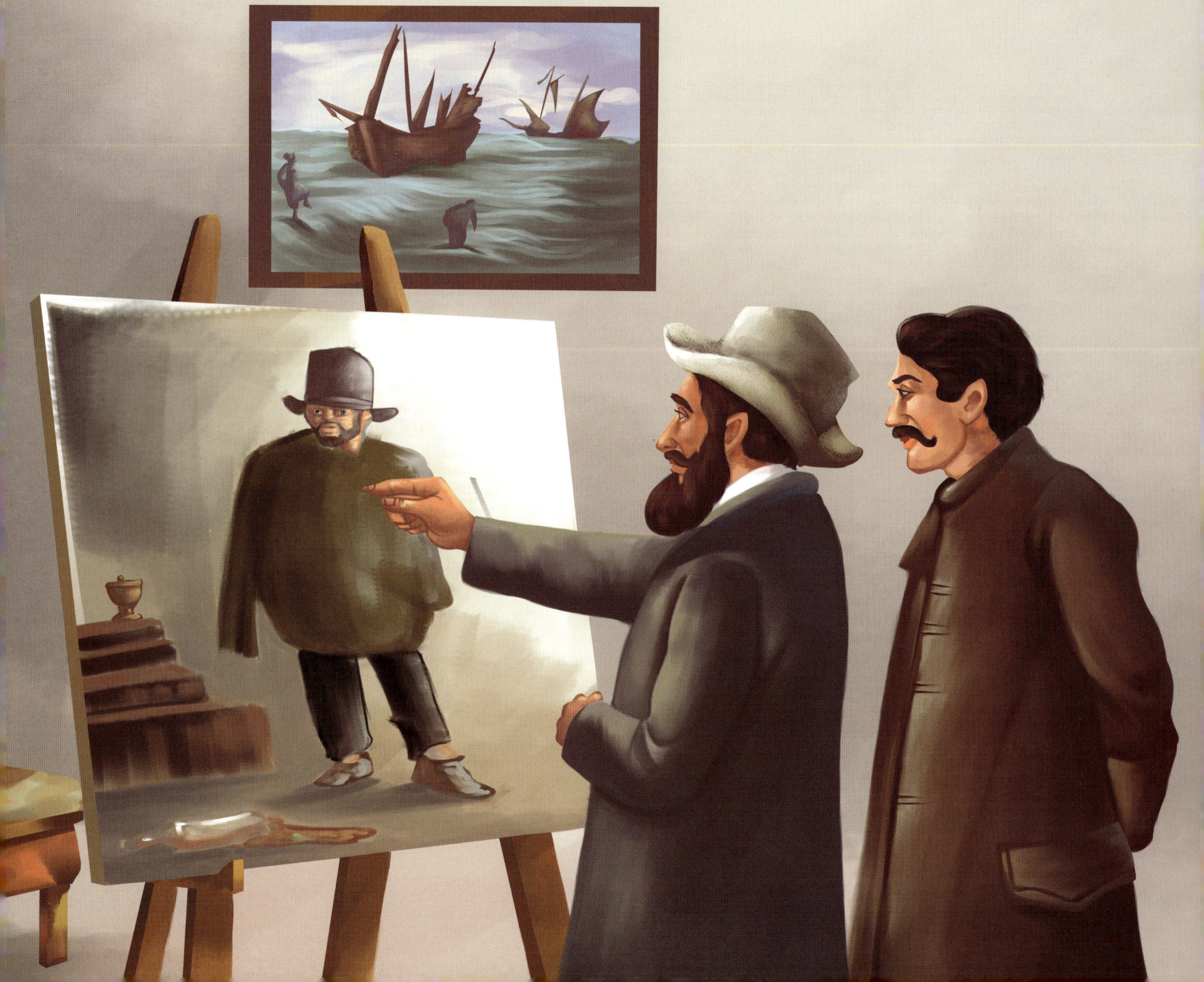

The next day, he showed his painting to Thomas Couture, his mentor whose studio Manet often worked in.

Couture gave a quick glance and dismissed the painting.

'Do some more,' he said.

As Manet was leaving he spotted the young model with a deep cleft in her chin and ginger-coloured hair. She was posing for Couture.

Manet found her very different from the regular Parisian models he painted.

He waited till she was done and followed her.

She entered a bar where she began to sing.

Manet could hardly contain his excitement; he knew he had to paint her. Not in the studio, but right here in the street or in the bar.

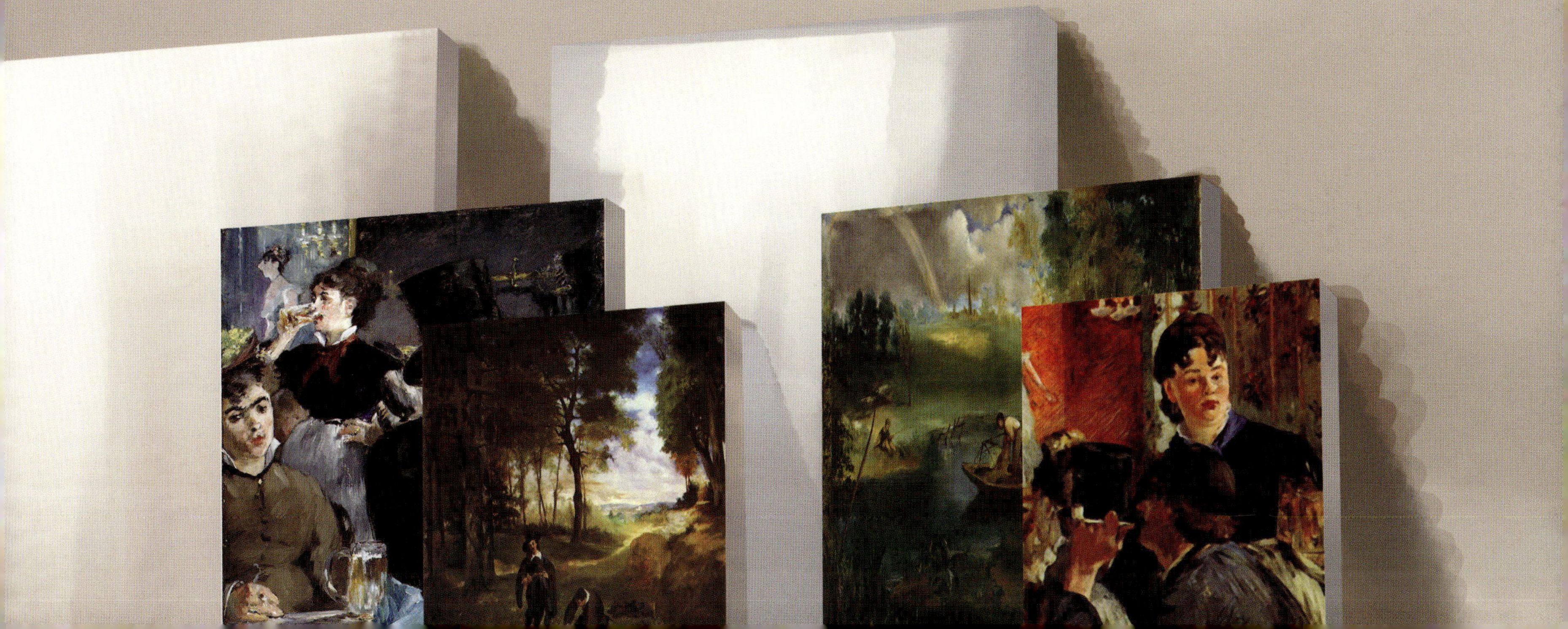

Manet waited outside the bar until she finished her singing.

The girl came outside and saw Manet waiting.

'You're Couture's student,' said the girl, 'I am Victorine. Why are you following me around?'

'Victorine, will you pose for me?' asked Manet.

'I have to pose for Couture and then I sing in the bar,' she said, 'I don't know.'

'I will make you famous,' said Manet, 'I will paint you like no one else can.'

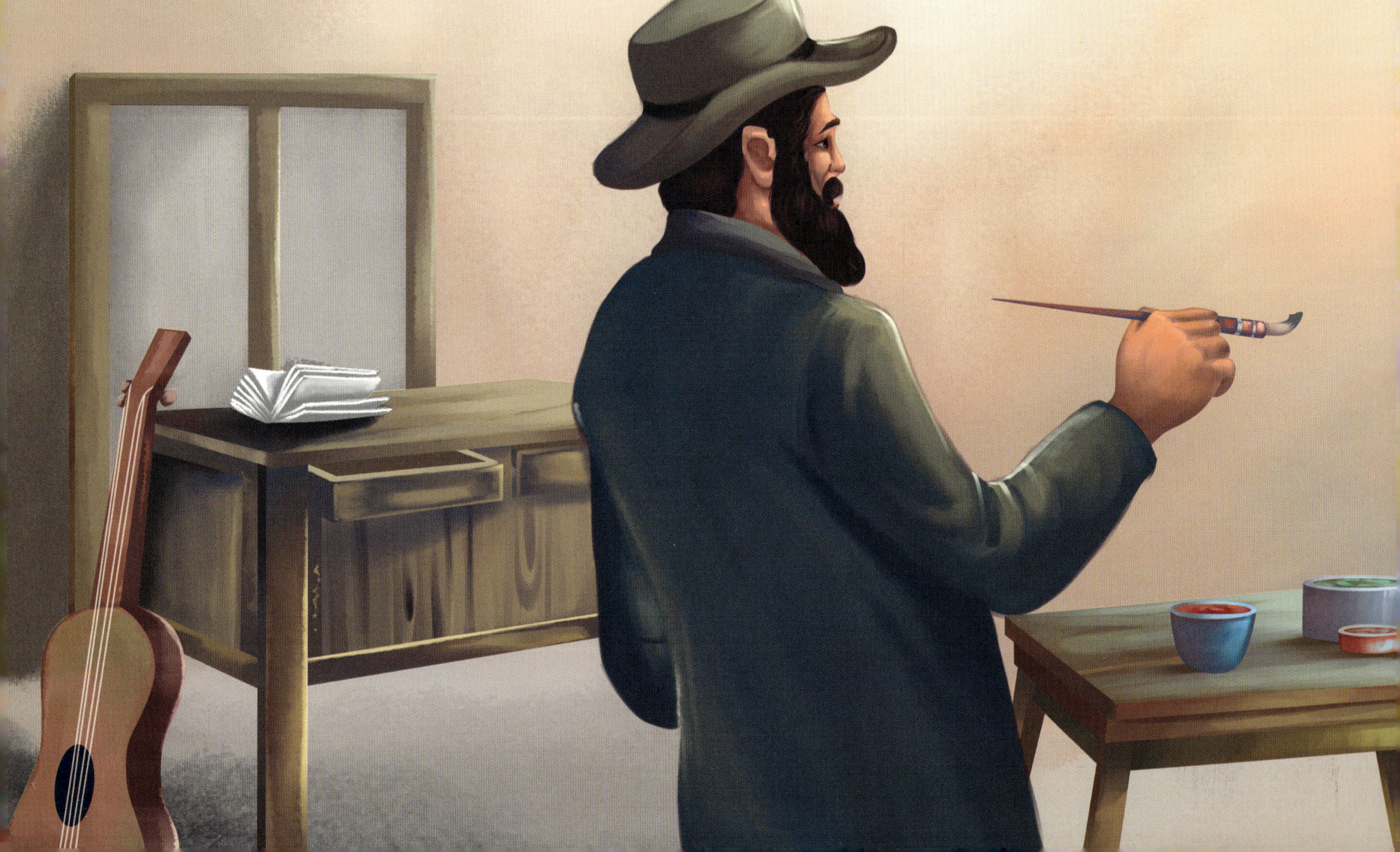

'Really? That is what they all say,' said Victorine.

Manet took her back to the studio and showed her *The Absinthe Drinker.*

'See, I want to paint people. People like you. In their everyday life,' said Manet.

Victorine found herself intrigued with this original young man.

He does have something, she thought.

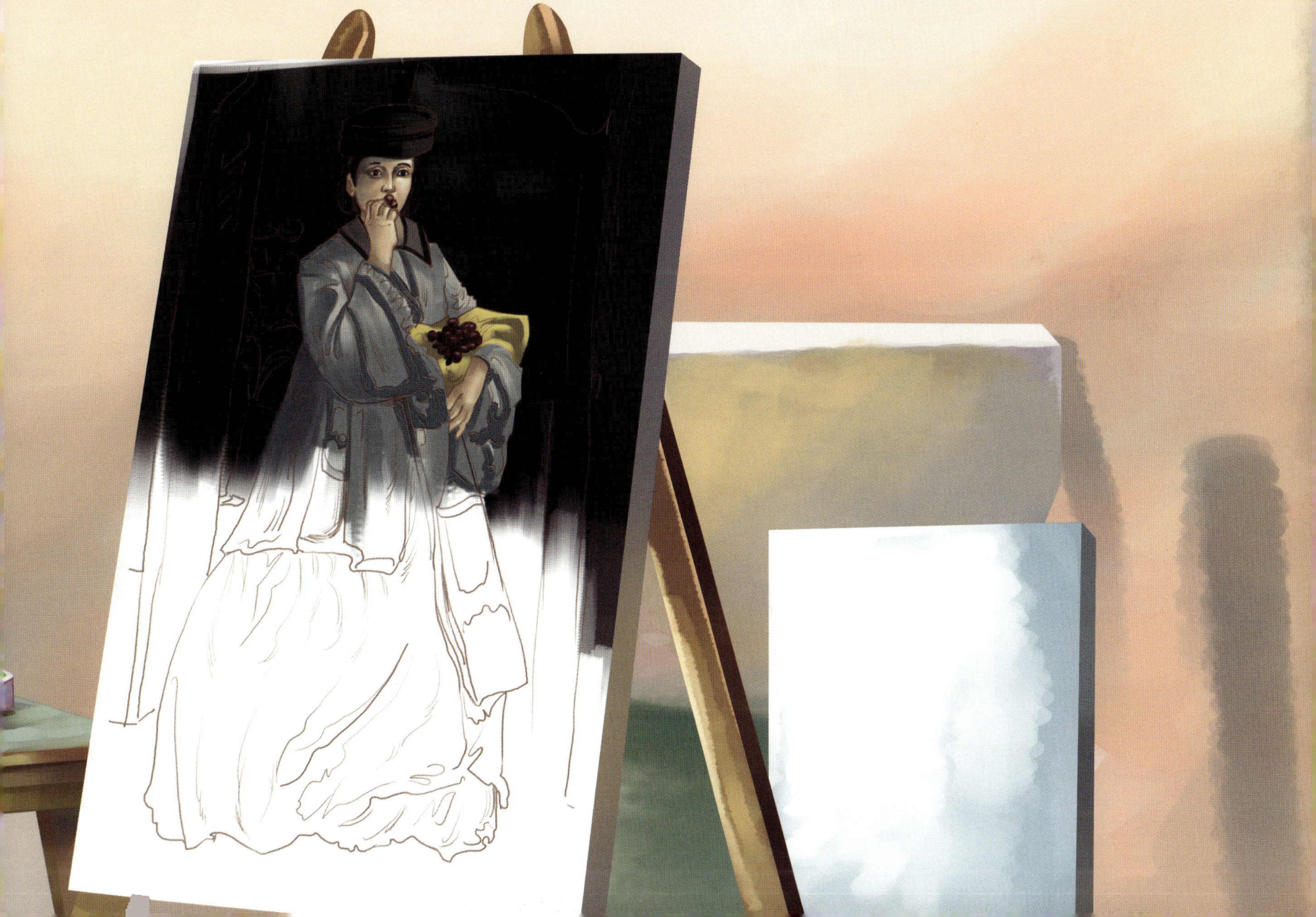

Victorine and Manet became friends. Both belonged to very different worlds, she was from a working class while he was from a wealthy family. But their connection to art drew them together.

"This painting of you, I am going to name it after you," said Manet.

Victorine was pleased. Nobody named paintings after their models.

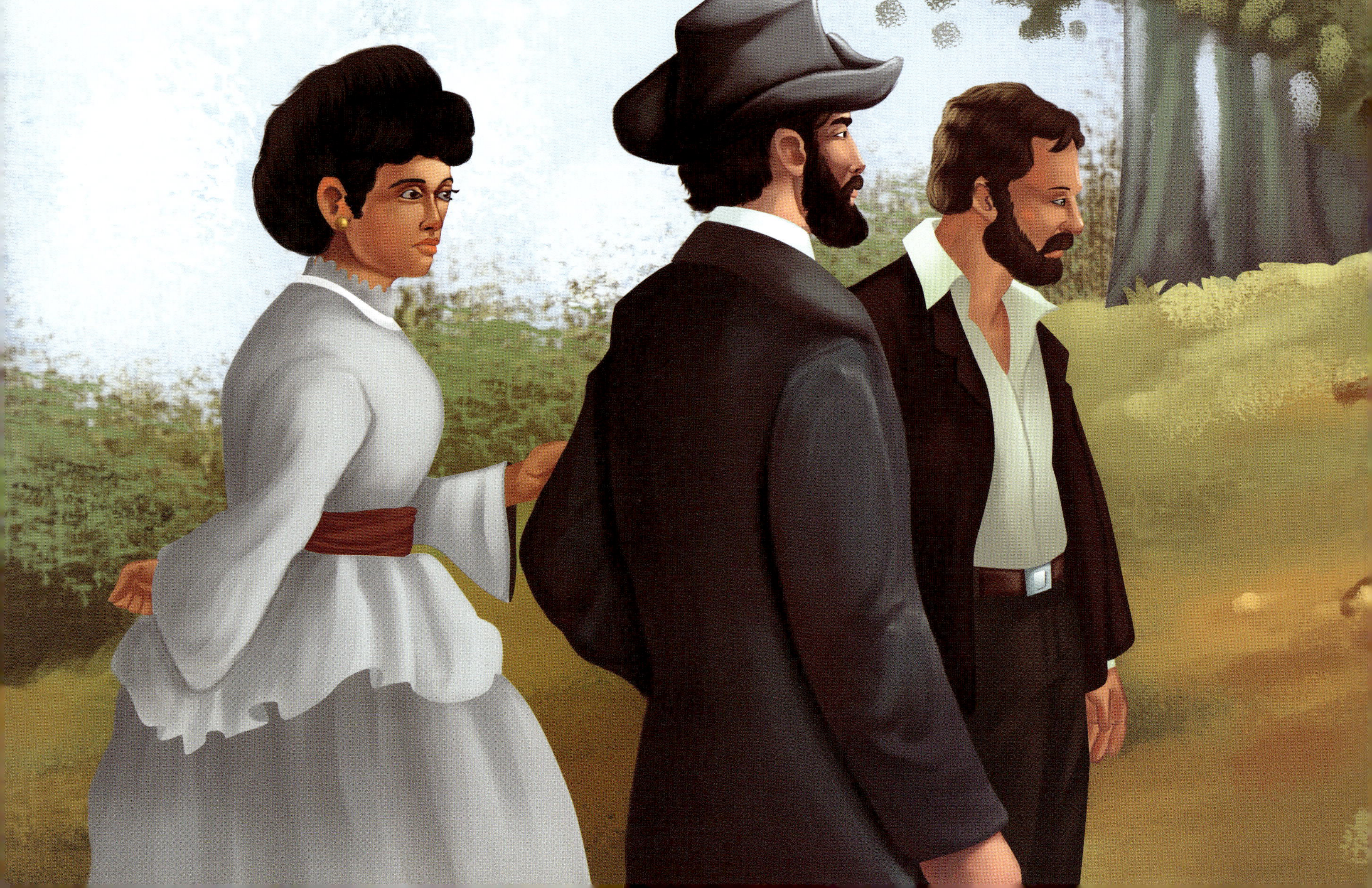

"I want to paint you in something that will shake Paris," said Manet. He had been thinking about how to get Victorine to agree to pose for it.

Charmed by his attention, Victorine agreed.

Manet unveiled *Le Dejeuner sur l'Herbe* the next day.

Even he was shocked by the response of the people.

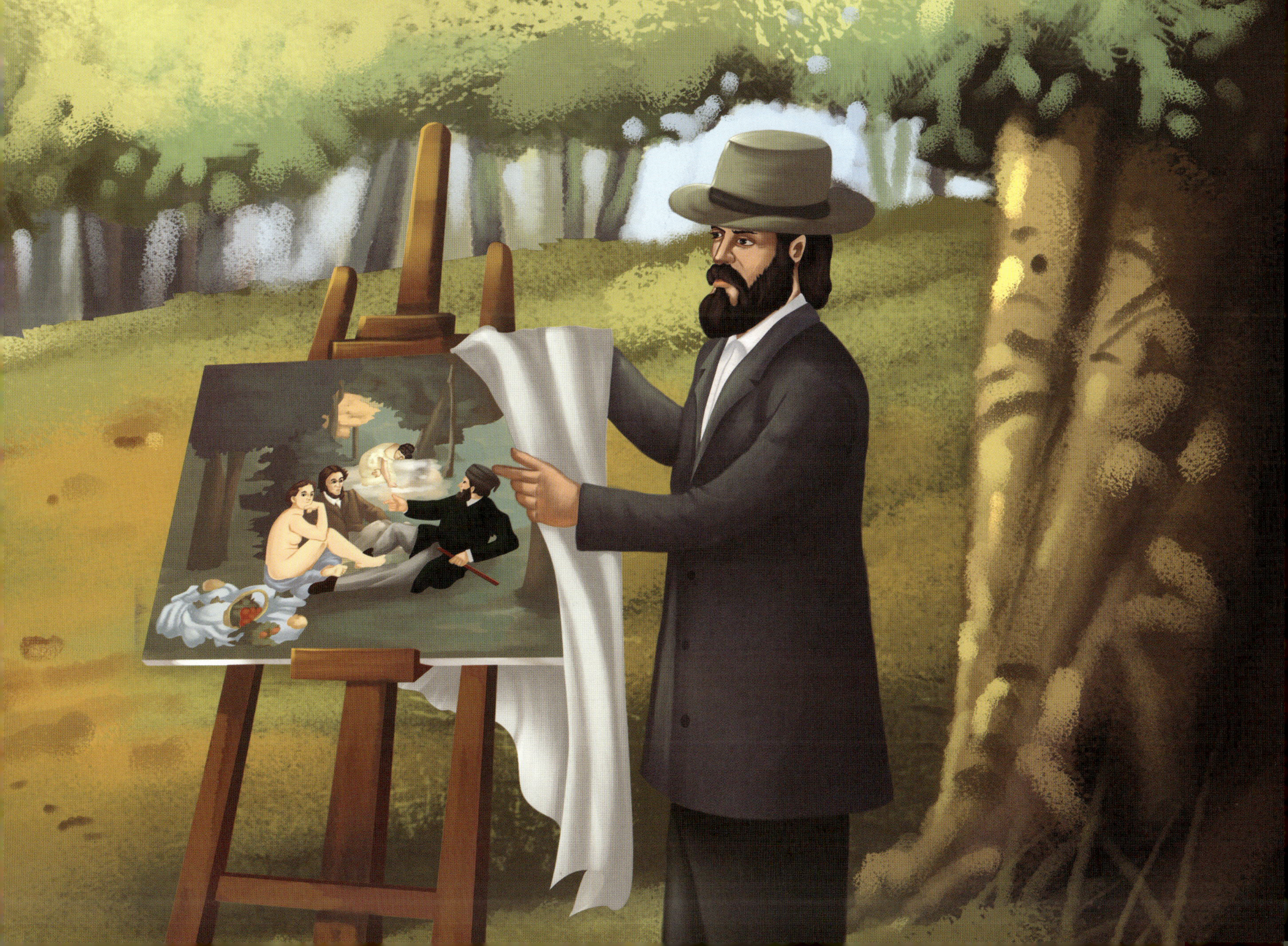

'I will not pose for you again,' said Victorine.

She had not been able to meet her friends as everyone was whispering about her scandalous painting.

'But I am making you famous!' said Manet.

'Famous by making a fool of me,' said Victorine.

'You knew what I was painting. How can you say that?'shouted back Manet.

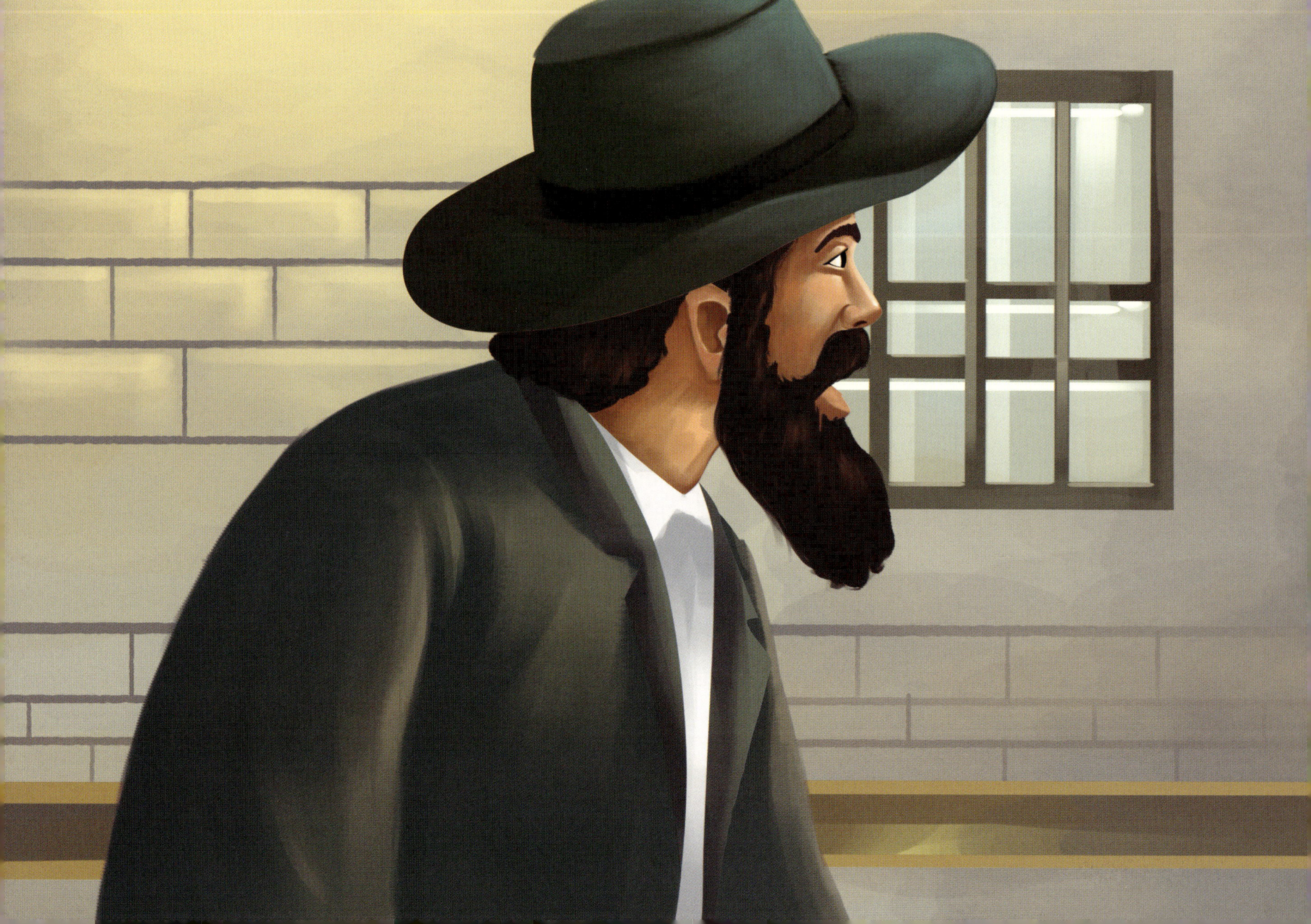

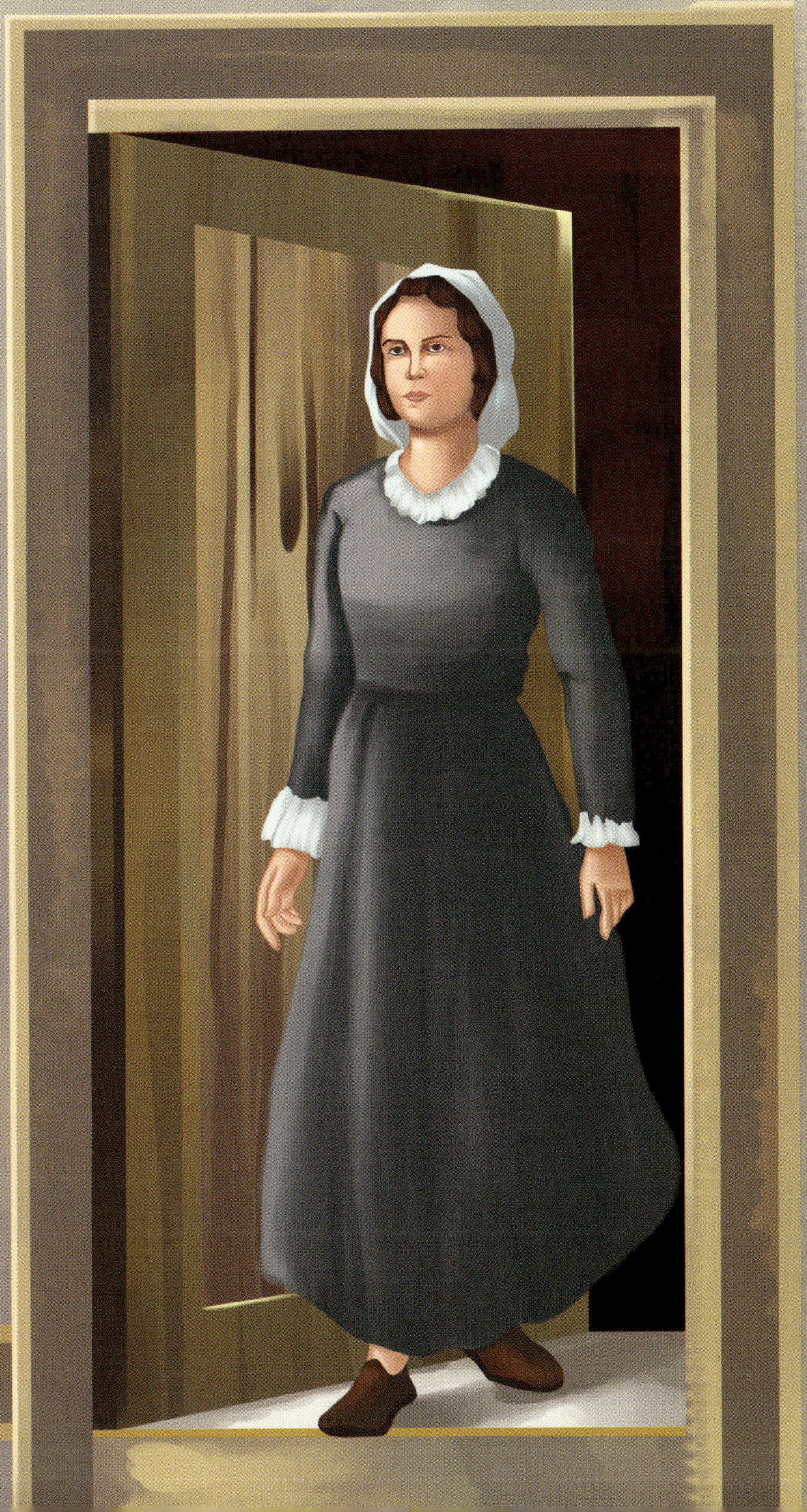

'I am not coming back,' said Victorine, storming out of Manet's studio.

Victorine had really enjoyed seeing Manet paint. She enrolled herself into a studio where she began to paint seriously.

One day, she found Manet waiting outside the studio.

'Victorine, I need you. Only you understand what I am trying to do,' he said.

Some months had passed so Victorine had calmed down. She had heard whispers that Manet was the only artist who was breaking the rules.

Victorine reluctantly agreed.

'This time you will not mess up,' she said.

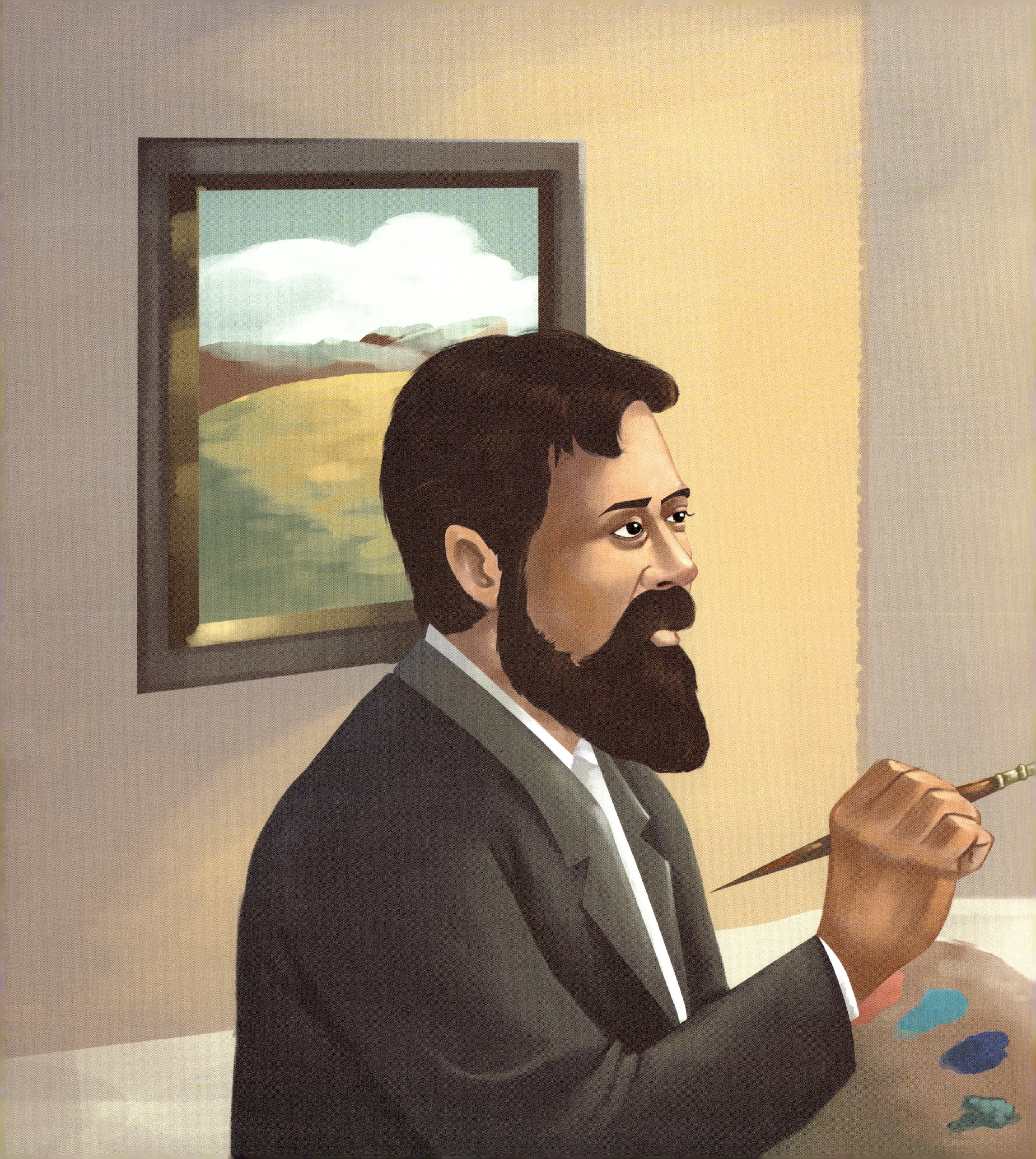

Manet continued to paint Victorine.

After a few years, Manet told Victorine, 'I have a painting in my head, I have to do it.'

Victorine knew Manet too well; she knew he must be thinking of something outrageous.

'Do you want to be remembered by history?' asked Manet.

Victorine knew she was making a mistake but she could not say no to Manet.

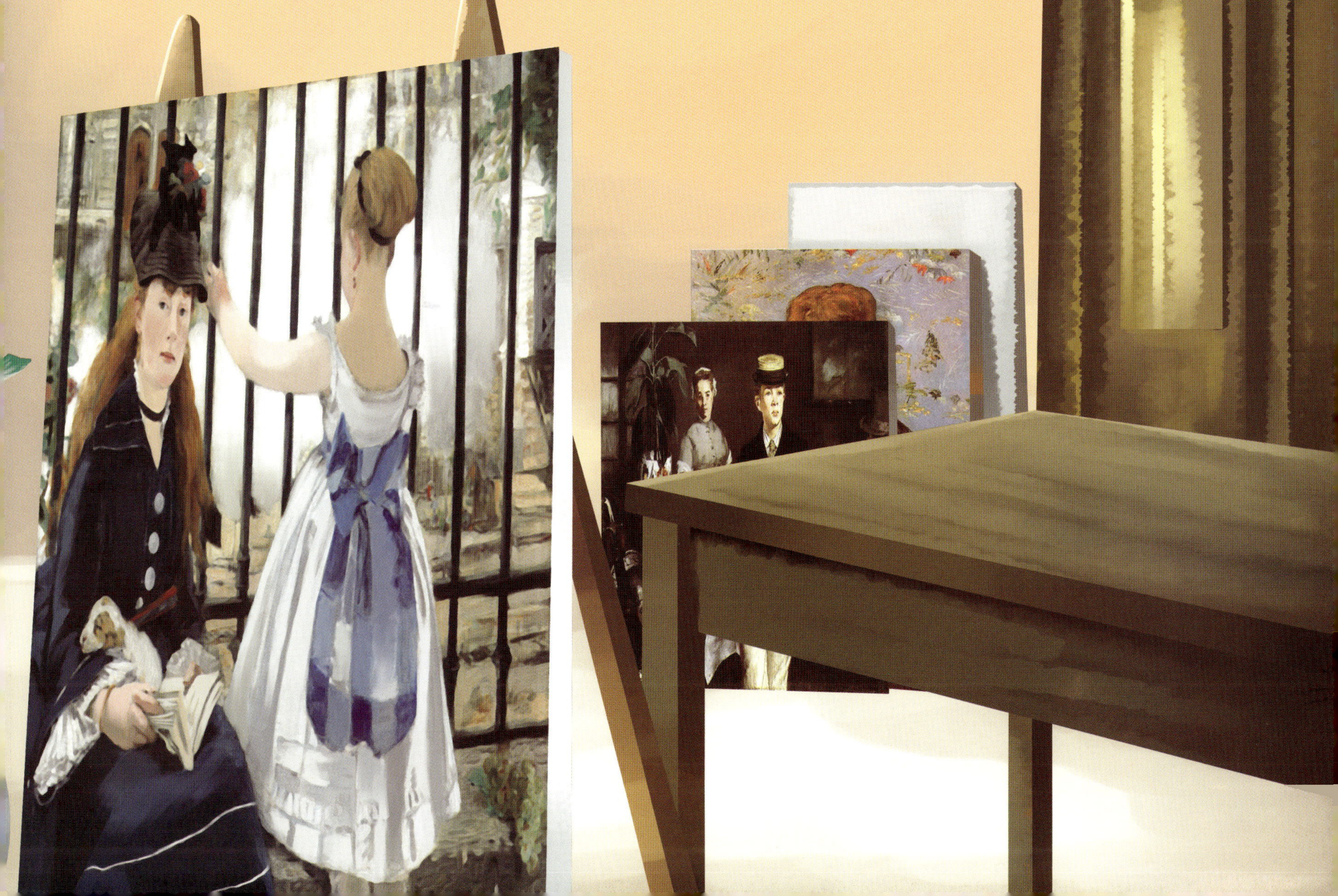

Manet painted her lying on the bed nude and named the painting *Olympia.*

When Manet unveiled the painting a few months later in Paris, 'Shocking!' said the papers.

Victorine looked at the papers in dismay.

'Victorine, listen to me,' said Manet but Victorine was busy packing some of the things she left in his studio.

'I think you and I are done,' she said, through her sobs.

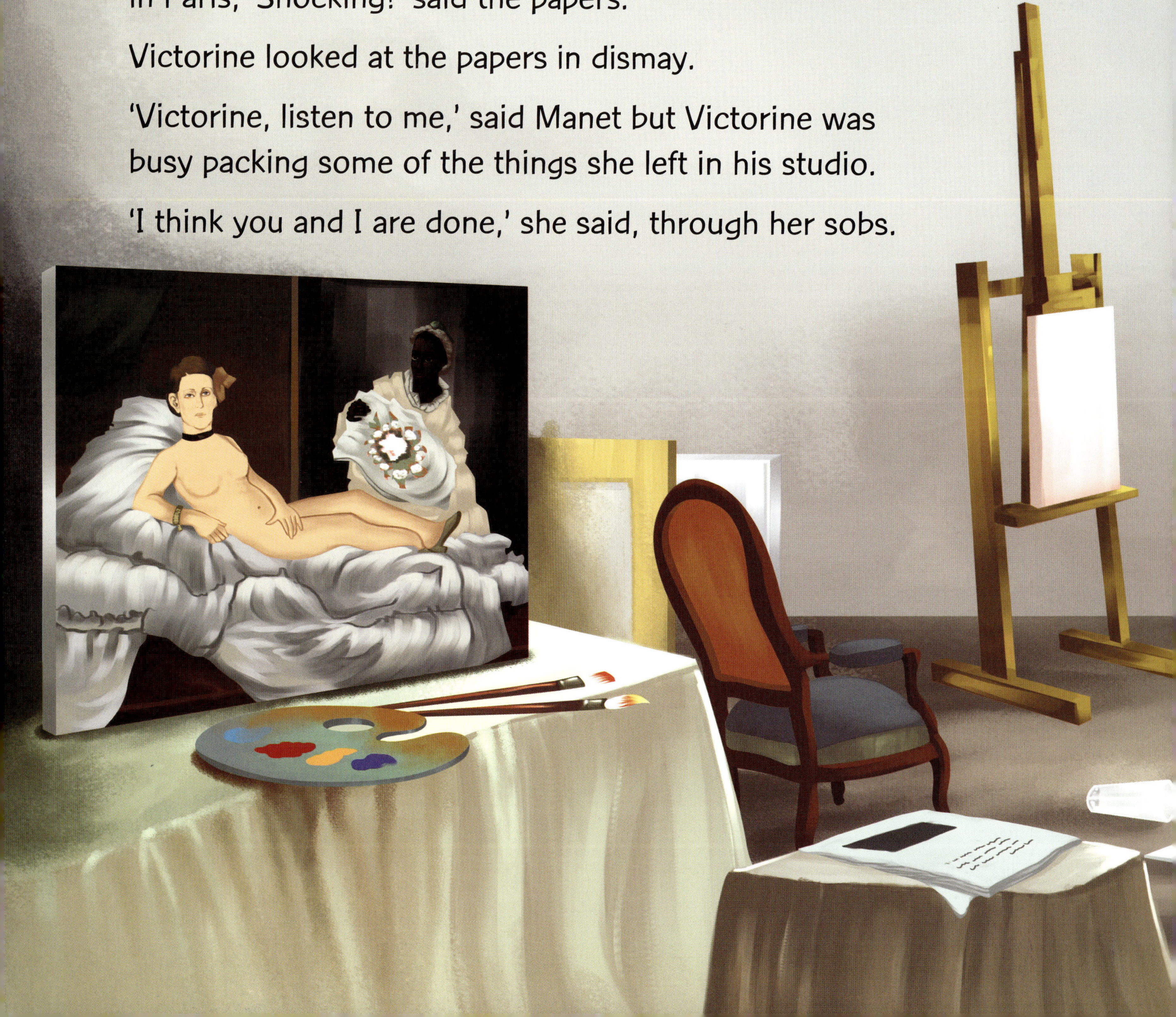

'Stop Victorine,'he said.

'Nothing happens to you. I am the one who has to suffer,' said Victorine.

She banged the door shut in Manet's face and walked out leaving Manet dejected at the door. He knew if he had to be true to his art, he would have to suffer the insults.

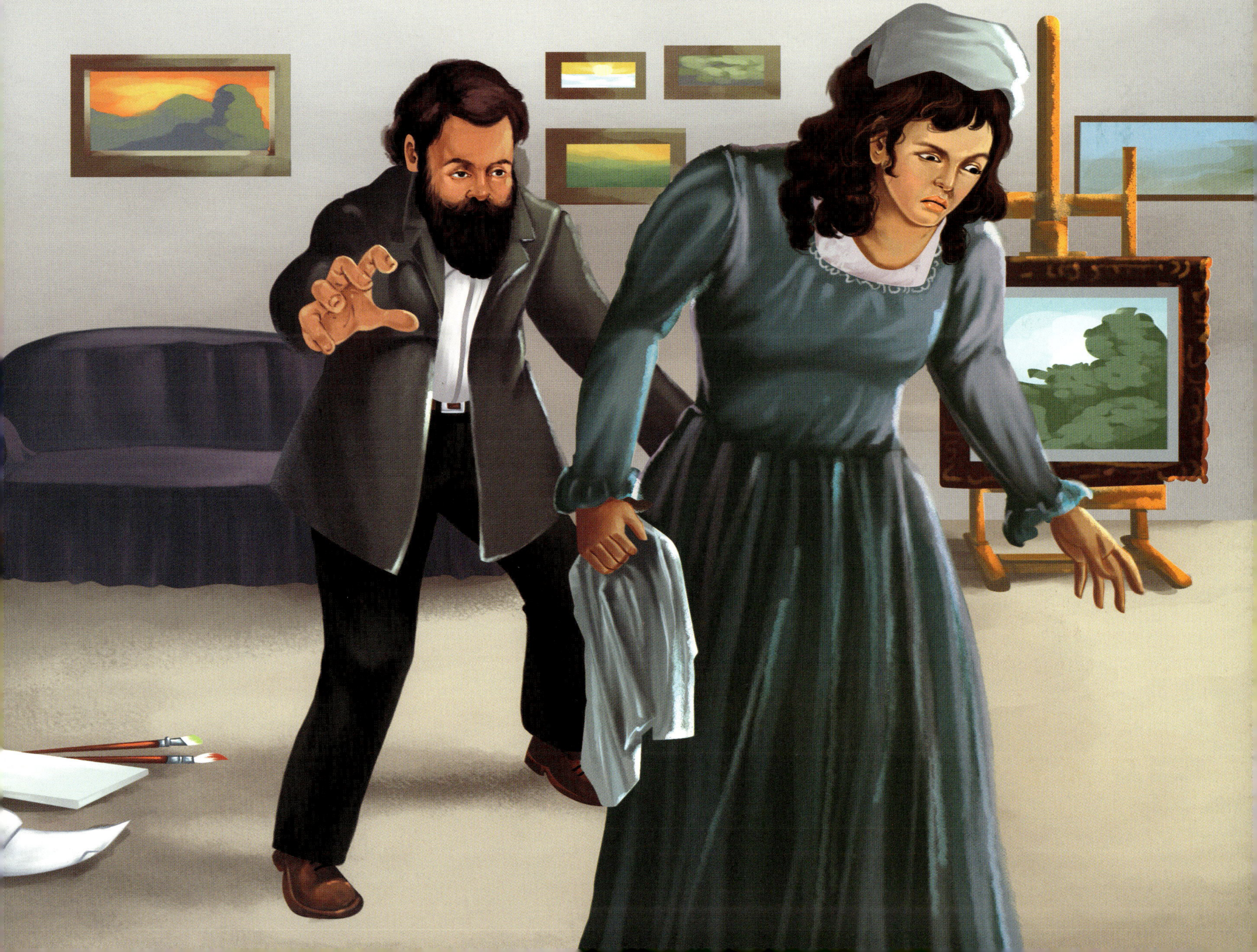

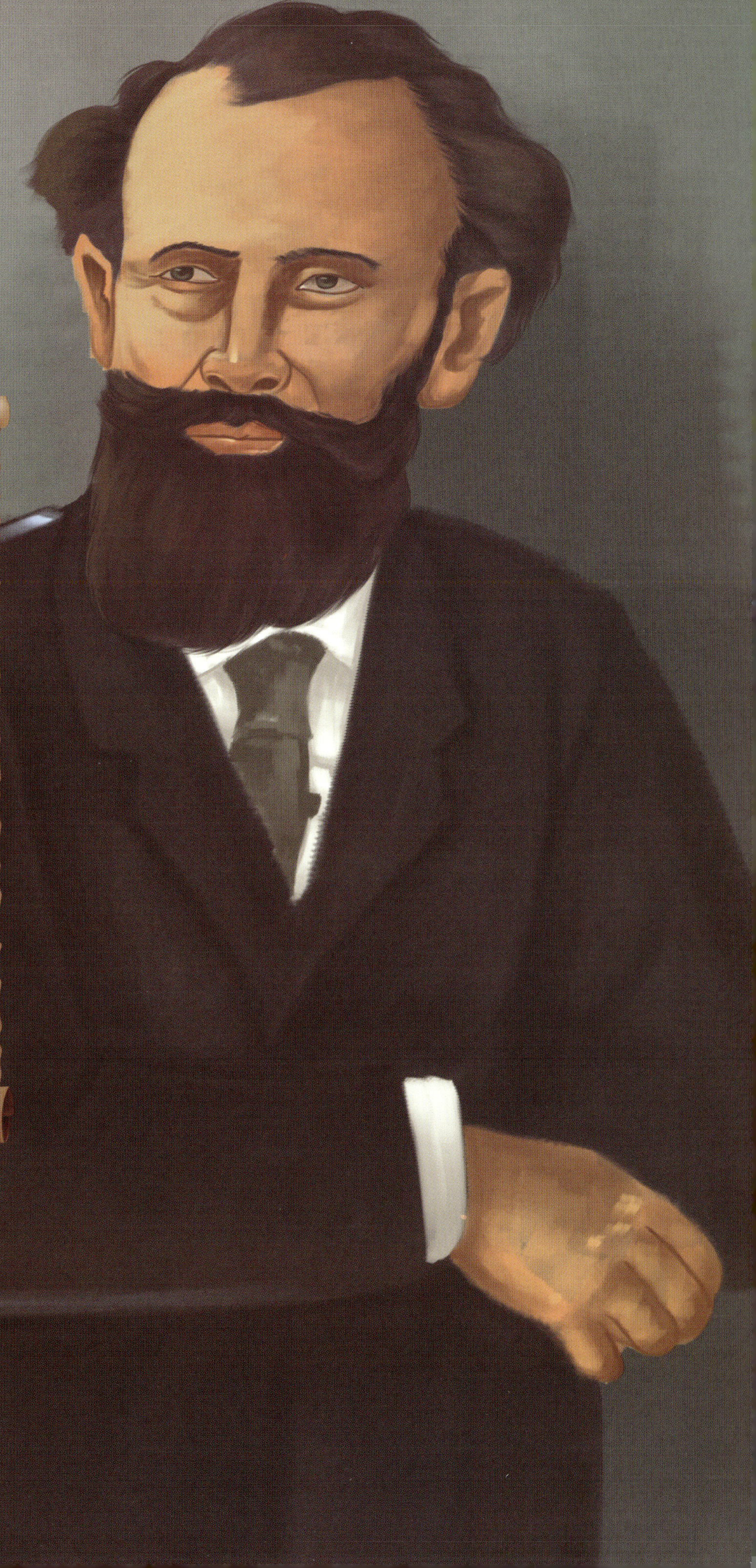

Édouard Manet was born in Paris in 1832 to wealthy parents.

In 1844, Manet studied law at the College Rollin.

In 1845, he started studying drawing at the insistence of his uncle, Charles Fournier.

In 1850 he joined Thomas Couture's painting studio for six years. He also registered as a copyist at the Louvre.

Manet set up his own studio in 1856.

In 1883, Manet fell sick and his left leg was amputated due to gangrene. He died of complications soon after.